WAH MING CHANG

Artist and Master of Special Effects

Gail Blasser Riley

—*Multicultural Junior Biographies*—

ENSLOW PUBLISHERS, INC.

44 Fadem Road
Box 699
Springfield, N.J. 07081
U.S.A.

P.O. Box 38
Aldershot
Hants GU12 6BP
U.K.

Library of Congress Cataloging-in-Publication Data

Riley, Gail Blasser.
Wah Ming Chang: artist and master of special effects / Gail Blasser Riley.
p. cm.—(Multicultural junior biographies)
Includes bibliographical references and index.
Summary: Examines the life of artist Wah Ming Chang, who is best known for his special effects for Disney films and the Star Trek series.
ISBN 0-89490-639-9
1. Chang, Wah—Juvenile literature. 2. Motion pictures—United States—Biography—Juvenile literature. 3. Artists—United States—Biography—Juvenile literature. [1. Chang, Wah. 2. Chinese Americans—Biography. 3. Artists.] I. Title. II. Series.
PN1998.3.C633R56 1995
792'.024'092—dc20
[B] 95-15390
CIP
AC

Printed in the United States of America

10 9 8 7 6 5 4 3 2 1

Illustration Credits: Courtesy of the J.H. Emerson Co., Cambridge, MA 02140, p. 45; Courtesy of Wah Ming Chang, pp. 9, 13, 15, 17, 18, 19, 21, 24, 32, 33, 35, 37, 41, 42, 50, 55, 58, 60, 61, 63, 67, 68, 70, 71, 76, 77, 81, 85, 87, 88, 89, 91; Peninsula School, Photo by Morley Baer, p. 25.

Cover Illustration: Courtesy of Wah Ming Chang

Contents

Dedication

This book is dedicated with admiration and respect to Glen and Wah Chang—two people who have selflessly given beauty, inspiration, delight, and an unparalleled sense of why we are all here on this Earth.

Acknowledgments

The author would like to offer special thanks to: My family—my husband Jim, and my children, Rachel, Jillian, and James, for caring, understanding, and supporting beyond support, even when my head didn't seem to be completely on my shoulders. Babs Bell Hajdusiewicz—for unending assistance in preparation of this manuscript, and for a heart, an ear, a phone, and a fax that were always open. Laurie Lazzaro Knowlton, for helping me get aboard the time machine. David Barrow, for showing me so eloquently the life's journey of a beautiful man. Robert H. Justman—without whom this book would not have been possible—for modestly showing me the past arena of tribbles, gorns, and communicators. Gene Warren, whose creativity, ebullience, and insight enriched my life and this book. Hank Ketcham, for a delightful look back to Dennis's big day at the park. Gary Lawrence, of Lawrence Galleries Portland, Oregon—for helping me experience the beauty of Wah's sculpture. Torben Deirup, for showing me the spotlights of puppet shows past. Lana Price, for helping me to see the brilliance of Wah at work. Hubert Rasbach, for offering such enlightening comments. Hope Duveneck, for showing me Wah's school days. Francis Duveneck, for taking me back to Peninsula School. Thanks also to graphic artist Chris MacGregor, for skill with illustrations.

An Artistic Marvel

On a sunny afternoon in 1925, people crowded to get into a busy San Francisco store. Some shouted and pointed. Others stood on tiptoe to get a better look. What was all the excitement about?

Children made their way to the front of the crowd and stepped inside. Near a store window, the children saw a San Francisco artist dressed in a cowboy suit. He stood beside a big machine.

The artist held pliers and a thin sheet of copper. Everyone watched as he rubbed a thick ink onto the copper plate. When he wiped the plate, ink stayed in special lines that had been

scraped into the copper. The lines formed a beautiful picture.

The young artist turned to the huge press machine beside him. He put the copper plate into the machine. His etching was almost complete.

The people of San Francisco were amazed by the artist. Some had even read about him in the newspaper.

"AN ARTISTIC MARVEL" — that's what newspaper reporters called Wah Ming Chang.[1] One article invited people to come see the young artist's work in a San Francisco gallery.

The visitors who came to see Wah Ming Chang's art could not have imagined the wonders that this "artistic marvel" would later create. In years to come, he would take millions of people on a journey through space, to a planet of apes, and back to an earth filled with dinosaurs. But these wonders were years away. In the 1920s, Wah Chang was just beginning his creative journey.

Wah Chang's love of art went far beyond his own creations. He spent many hours showing *others* how to create beautiful art. Wah gave lessons to the people who came to admire his work at the galleries.

—Wide World Photo.

EXPERT ARTIST—At age of 9 is Wah Ming Chang, San Francisco Chinese boy. Blanding Sloan, well known artist, has taught him elements and he has learned to draw, make etched plate and do actual printing. Wah Ming Chang inherited his talent from father and mother, both artists and designers.

L. A. Illustrated Daily News
Feb. 7, 1927.

Wah's photograph appeared in a 1927 Los Angeles newspaper.

Those who came for art lessons might have expected their teacher to be an adult. But the artist they had come to learn from was not an adult. He was not even in his teens. In fact, he had not even reached his ninth birthday. This artist, called a "genius," was an eight-year-old boy dressed in a cowboy suit.[2]

How would the talent of this eight-year-old unfold? How would he shape the future? How would his talents explode onto television and movie screens around the world? How would he use his art to reach out to others as he fought to overcome the hardship of a crippling disease? And, how would Wah Ming Chang's creative journey take him in the direction of time travel, *Star Trek* monsters, and academy-award-winning special effects?

Dragons and Puppets

When Wah Ming Chang was a very young boy, he was not yet creating monsters, puppets, and time machines. Still, his mother could see his talent.

In 1919, two-year-old Wah liked to draw pictures of lambs.[1] He delighted in slipping these early works of art under his mother's pillow to surprise her.[2] Wah spent many happy hours with his mother, Fai Sue Chang. Fai Sue had graduated from the California School of Arts and Crafts. She was a talented artist, actress, and clothing designer.[3]

Fai Sue did not give Wah any formal art

lessons. But she always had art supplies handy. Wah put these supplies to good use.

The Tea Room

Young Wah spent many hours at his family's tea room. The Ho Ho tea room was on the top floor of a building on Sutter Street in San Francisco. Wah's parents, Fai Sue and Dai Song Chang, cooked the food and served their customers.

Wah often sat quietly in a corner of the tea room sketching pictures on the backs of menus. All around him, colorful Chinese lanterns hung from the ceiling. Beautiful works of art lined the walls, and the delightful aroma of hot tea and tasty Chinese food filled the air.

The tea room hummed with the conversation of San Francisco artists, writers, and musicians. Some of them were famous. Others struggled to make enough money to live. Wah's mother welcomed them all.[4]

Wah spent many hours riding up and down the elevator to the tea room. A Scottish man operated the elevator. He and Wah became good friends.

On Wah's eighth birthday, the "elevator

Many artists, actors, and musicians visited the Ho Ho Tea Room. Wah's mother, Fai Sue Chang, welcomed the customers and friends.

man" gave him a special gift. Wah opened the package to find just what he had always wanted — a pair of chaps. Wah liked the leather coverings that a cowboy straps over the front of his pants. And now he could be like a real cowboy!

Wah loved cowboys.[5] He wore his cowboy

suit nearly every day. He waited in long lines to see his favorite cowboy movies.

Five-year-old Wah also liked to fly kites, play marbles, and read.[6] He would often go to Gilbert's Bookstore, across the street from the tea room. There he liked to sit on a bottom shelf with a book in his hands.

Wah enjoyed spending time in Harry Livingston's art studio. He sometimes sat as a model while the art students drew pictures of him.[7] Harry Livingston, the studio owner, often challenged Wah to a lively game of chess.

Wah attended an American school. He also spent many hours in a Chinese school. But he had a hard time there. He had forgotten most of the Chinese he had spoken when he was very young. And he didn't understand the lessons.[8]

"World's Youngest Etcher"

Wah loved working with art.[9] He was encouraged by the many artists who visited the tea room.

One day, seven-year-old Wah sat quietly sketching. Well-known artist Blanding Sloan watched in amazement. Sloan had designed sets and lighting for Broadway shows. He was so

CHINESE BOY, 8, ARTIST 'FIND'
IN S. F. SALON WITH FAMOU

Wah had made many character sketches by the time he was eight years old. He appears in this newspaper photograph with his mother.

impressed with Wah's talent that he invited the child to become one of his select students. Sloan called his select students "associates."[10]

Young Wah Ming Chang quickly earned the respect of Sloan's other associates. This was unusual because Wah was the only child working at the studio.[11]

Wah carefully watched the other artists. He was most interested in their etchings. He couldn't wait to make an etching of his own![12]

So one day, Wah waited until everyone had left the studio. He did not want to be laughed at when he first tried his hand at etching. The young artist handled the nitric acid, needles, and hot wax with care. He knew that an etcher's tools could be very dangerous. He followed the etching process, step-by-step. And his first attempt was a success!

Before Wah was even nine years old, a San Francisco newspaper would call him the "world's youngest etcher."[13]

Blanding Sloan soon became like a father to Wah. Wah's parents had grown busier and busier with their work. And Wah had begun spending more and more time with Sloan and his wife, Mildred Taylor.

Sloan's painting of Wah appears on the left. On the right is a charcoal sketch of Wah by Sloan.

Sloan really liked Wah.[14] The two went to movies together, played horseshoes, and often just sat and talked.

In the art studio, Sloan gave Wah "complete freedom in his choice of medium, style, and subject matter." If Wah wanted to paint a cowboy, he painted a cowboy. If he wanted to

etch a dog, he etched a dog. If he wanted to draw an abstract, something that didn't look quite real, that's exactly what he did.[15]

Sloan taught Wah about many types of art. Sloan also made Wah part of his own art. He painted a portrait of the young artist in a cowboy suit, with a dragon in the background. Later, Wah would create many dragons of his own.

Sharing Art

Blanding Sloan introduced Wah to the fine art of puppet making and puppet theater. Puppets would one day become a very important part of Wah's life.

At the age of seven, Wah made several guest visits to a San Francisco radio show. On *Mac and the Kiddies Gang*, he told stories and sang songs.[16]

By 1925, Wah

THE SAN FRANCISCO CALL AND POST • • Cal

RADIO

Here are "Mac" and his gang, who are making a big hit with the kiddies of radioland with their stories and songs during the new children's hour broadcast from 5:30 to 6:30 every night over the City of Paris-Call station, KFRC. Left to right are "Mac," "Stub," the dog; Blanding Sloan, who writes the children's stories, and below, Wah Chang

Wah enjoys his pedal car as he appears with others from a radio show.

Ming Chang had become a well-known artist. But this radio show guest and "world's youngest etcher" was still a child. He liked to pedal up and down the sidewalks of San Francisco in his little car. The car been a gift from a department store owner who was impressed by Wah's talent.[17]

By the time he was eight, Wah's artwork was on display at a downtown San Francisco art gallery. There, he shyly told reporters, "I think I'd

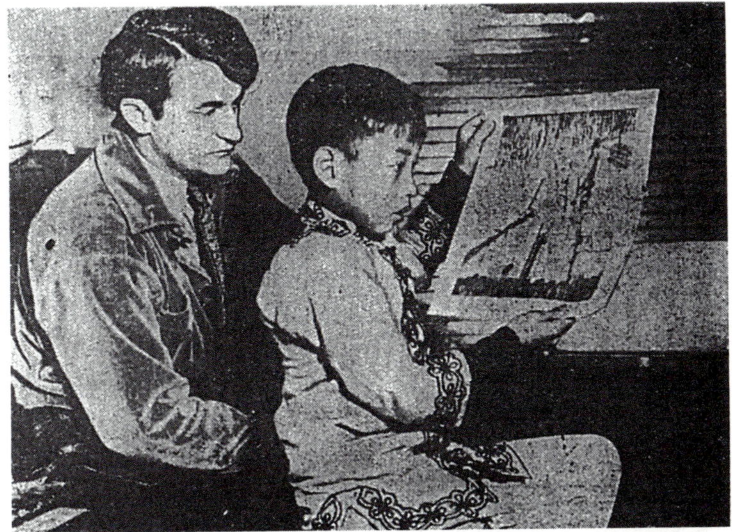

Prints of Arts—Preparations are being made today at the Palace of the Legion of Honor for the exhibit of block prints and etchings by Blanding Sloan from February 5 to 28. In the photo the artist himself and Wah Meng Chang, nine, are looking over one of the prints. Chang understands and does the whole process of etching. A special invitation has been issued to teachers and school children to visit the exhibit at 11 a. m., February 11.

Wah Chang and Blanding Sloan prepare for an art exhibition.

rather draw cowboys and Indians and houses and things like that, and when I grow up, I'm going to be an artist. You'll see."[18]

Wah's talent took the country by storm. When he was eleven years old, newspaper headlines read: "Wah Ming Chang Hailed as Genius With Brush; Has Exhibited in Leading United States Cities."[19] But all the genius in the world could not keep tragedy and sadness from young Wah's life.

A Great Loss

No one told Wah that his mother was sick. He only knew that she had gone away to visit a friend. Wah did not see his mother for weeks.

It was a warm San Francisco afternoon when Blanding Sloan took eleven-year-old Wah for a walk in Golden Gate Park. Sloan had to break the terribly sad news. As the two sat side-by-side in the sunshine, Sloan explained to Wah that he would not see his mother again. She had died. Wah cried. He cried so hard that a person in the park stopped to see if Sloan might be harming the child. And Sloan had to explain Wah's grief to the stranger.[20]

Wah lost his mother when he was only eleven years old. This photograph of Fai Sue Chang appeared in the newspaper after her death.

San Franciscans mourned Fai Sue Chang's death. A newspaper story said:

> One of the lovable . . . characters of San Francisco . . . whose death will bring sorrow to the hearts of scores of [people]. It sometimes happens in the career of an artist that pictures don't sell. Work doesn't come always for the asking. Funds and spirits get low. Those customers of the tea room who have experienced such misfortune remember Fai Sue as a sort of fairy godmother.[21]

Many, many people would miss the thoughtful, loving Sue Chang. However, no one would ever feel the loss in quite the same way as Wah.

Wah's father seemed to lose interest in the tea room after the death of his wife. "He wanted to travel as far away from the hurt of his loss as he could possibly go."[22] Dai Song Chang made plans to travel—alone—to Europe.

School Days

Dai Song Chang asked Blanding Sloan and his wife, Mildred Taylor, to become Wah's guardians. Dai Song wanted them to take his son into their home and care for him like parents. Blanding and Mildred welcomed the idea.[1]

Wah loved living in the Sloan/Taylor home. He says, "In a way, I related to Blanding more than [to] my father. He [Sloan] was very child-like in some respects. He knew how to relate to kids."[2]

In the art studio, Sloan related to Wah with trust and faith. "He never [gave] any criticism as part of teaching me how to draw or what to

An Artist At Seven

Wah Ming Chang, world's youngest etcher, who also likes to play cowboy, fly kites and shoot marbles the same as Occidental boys. But he's a prodigy in art. Blanding Sloan, his teacher, is shown in the background.

Blanding Sloan took Wah under his wing after Wah's mother passed away. This newspaper clipping from the 1920s shows Blanding Sloan watching Wah lift an etching from an etching press.

draw. He would just tell me how to do it . . . and I think he always treated me with confidence that I could do these things."[3]

Wah got along well with Sloan's wife. She was a writer for a newspaper and her ideas were unusual for her time. Through her writing, Mildred Taylor had encouraged equal rights for women. Few people had the courage to express such an idea in the 1920s.[4] And Taylor had chosen to keep her own last name when she and Blanding Sloan married. Such a thing was almost unheard of at the time!

Wah's happiness at the Sloan/Taylor home was interrupted early when he was admitted to a special hospital. Wah was in poor health. A lung disease called tuberculosis was making many people sick during the 1920s. "I spent

almost a year in a sanitarium . . . I didn't have tuberculosis, but . . . I guess I could have been [likely to get] it."[5]

Haunted Houses

After Wah came home from the hospital, he received a scholarship to attend . . . a "haunted house!" At least that's what students called the Peninsula School of Creative Education in Menlo Park, California.

The Peninsula School building was a huge

Wah received a scholarship to attend the Peninsula School in Menlo Park, California. Some called it a "haunted house."

home surrounded by trees. The mansion had originally been built by a Mr. Coleman for his bride. But Mr. Coleman's bride never had a chance to live in her new home. Rumor had it that she drowned on her honeymoon.[6]

Wah and his classmates had heard that the bride's ghost often sobbed in the attic. Daring students would sometimes creep up the mansion stairs to see for themselves. Frightened, the children would then race to slide down the banister to escape.

The Peninsula School was not like most schools of its time. Parents had started the school because they wanted a new, creative way for their children to learn. At the Peninsula School, students had a great deal of freedom. They were encouraged to express their curiosity and to use their talents.[7]

Wah made two rings in the school's metal shop. Many years later, the rings would be a gift for his wife. Wah also made a leather coin purse for Mildred Taylor. He put her initials on the purse. Everyone laughed at the initials, M.T. They said that the purse was often just that—empty![8]

While studying at the Peninsula School, Wah

teamed up with his friend Torben Deirup. The two created many unique, professional puppet shows. He and Torben put on shows for classmates and others.

Today, Deirup remembers those puppet shows very well: "I was very good with my hands. I could build almost anything, but Wah's ability was superior. Though his hands were much smaller than mine, they were strong and nimble. It was a beautiful thing to watch him carve."[9]

Wah and Torben built a portable stage for their puppet shows. The stage had footlights and spotlights. Deirup remembers one special show: "We had a haunted house, complete with thunder and lightning and wind machines."[10]

Puppets, Dummies, and Practical Jokes

Wah and Torben did not limit their creativity to formal productions. They sometimes used their talent to play jokes. Once, they made a life-size dummy of a man. They put the dummy in the gutter in front of the house across the street from Torben's home. Then they raced to Torben's attic and peeked out the window.

Torben's neighbors came out of their house. They looked toward the dummy, then raced back inside. Wah remembers thinking neighbors must have run inside to call police.[11] Wah and Torben ran out and grabbed the dummy. The three made a quick getaway. By the time police arrived, there was not a shred of evidence.

Wah and Torben played many other jokes with their realistic-looking "man." Sometimes, they would lean the "man" against a car in a driveway. Then they would ring the doorbell and dash into the bushes.

But finally, Wah and Torben played one joke too many. They were caught with the dummy! Torben remembers it well. "We received an official note from the chief of police . . . If that dummy was ever seen on the streets of Palo Alto again, it would be reform school for us!"[12]

Many years later, Wah Chang would create another dummy—one that wouldn't have problems with police. Wah's dummy of Donald Duck would be seen across the country on the knee of Ducky Nash, the man who spoke for Donald Duck in cartoons.

Dance Lessons

The Peninsula School was far from Wah's home with Blanding Sloan and Mildred Taylor. So Wah lived with a teacher for a while. When the teacher moved away, Wah went to live with Torben Deirup's grandmother.

On school days, Wah arrived for classes on his bike in the morning. Many of his classmates stepped out of fancy cars driven by special drivers. Some of Wah's classmates were very wealthy. But this didn't affect Wah's relationship with his classmates. No matter how he arrived at school, he was well-liked.[13]

Still, things were not always easy for Wah. When he was thirteen, he and Torben signed up to take a dance class. Wah had only attended a few times. Then one day before class began, he was asked to leave and not come back. Wah remembers, "I felt badly . . . I remember sitting outside . . . dressed up while other students came in."[14]

Torben wondered why his friend had stopped coming to dance class. He later learned that some of the girls' parents were furious when they found out that their daughters were dancing with a Chinese boy.[15]

Though it has been more than sixty years, Deirup remembers the dance class incident well. He is still angry about this 1930s event. "The idea that anybody could discriminate against somebody like Wah, I just couldn't imagine it!" [16]

On the Way to Walt Disney Studios

When Wah left the Peninsula School, he left behind something very special. Children at the school were invited to paint their huge artistic creations on the walls.

These masterpieces were allowed to remain for only one year. Then they were "washed away to allow for fresh inspiration."[1]

Still, there was one picture that *was* allowed to remain year after year. School director Frances Duveneck explained why. "It [the picture] was by our gifted Chinese pupil, Wah Chang. He painted a life-size portrait of a great buckskin mare with flowing mane and tail, standing with her newborn

Wah painted this mural on the wall of the Peninsula School.

colt in front of an old wooden barn which everyone recognized as the 'Hidden Villa' barn. When this masterpiece had to be washed away, some of us had tears in our eyes."[2]

In years to come, Wah's talents would be captured in many more masterpieces—these works would remain forever.

"The Snail"

After leaving the Peninsula School, Wah moved to Hollywood. He again lived with Blanding Sloan and Mildred Taylor. They now had a four-year-old son.

Over the years, Sloan and Wah often traveled together. They especially enjoyed going hunting and fishing.[3] Wah had never done such things with his own father. In 1934, Sloan, Wah, and Wah's dog Bing took to the road.[4] They traveled in a mobile home that looked like an art studio

inside. At a very young age, Wah had named this movable studio "The Snail," because "like a snail, [it] carries a house on its back."[5]

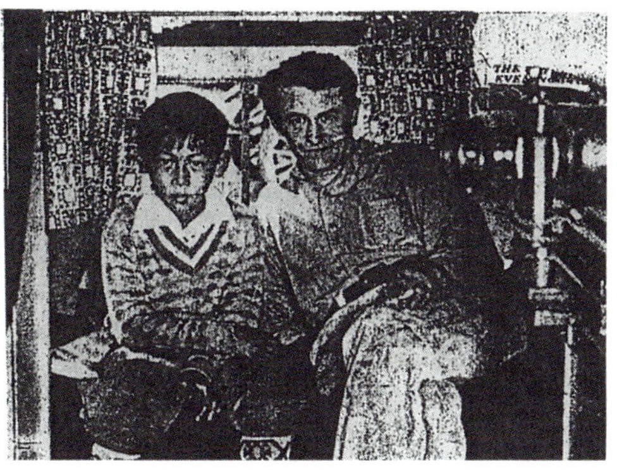

In this old snapshot from Wah Ming Chang's scrapbook, Wah and Sloan sit inside "The Snail."

Wah made good use of "The Snail" throughout the years. When Sloan and Wah were not traveling, the mobile home sat in Sloan's driveway. Wah lived in "The Snail" while in high school.

When Wah was sixteen, Sloan trusted him with a great responsibility.[6] Sloan had been hired to do the sets for two shows in the Hollywood Bowl. He gave Wah the job of building the sets for *The Victory Ball Ballet.* Wah says:

> I feel very proud that I was able to do that at the age of sixteen, and look back on it with some wonderment that Blanding gave a young boy the responsibility of building these sets. The sets for the ballet had to be . . . moved into place . . . in the dark by the dancers themselves. Fortunately, everything worked out all right, but when I think of it, I'm amazed that it worked.[7]

During Wah's high school years, the United States was in the middle of the Great Depression, a very difficult time following World War I. Money was scarce and many people were without jobs. Wah says, "While we never missed a meal, it was always a problem of the rent money, or the phone bill or other utilities."[8]

The Cavalcade of Texas

In 1936, when Wah Chang was eighteen, the state of Texas planned *The Texas Centennial Fair,* a big celebration of the Lone Star state's one-hundredth birthday. One of the main attractions was *The Cavalcade of Texas*, a spectacular outdoor play. The play showed one-hundred years of Texas history. Sloan, who was from Texas, was in charge of the lighting for the *Cavalcade*. He also became the show's director.

By this time, eighteen-year-old Wah Chang had finished high school. He joined Sloan in Dallas, Texas, as a *Cavalcade* staff artist. Chang painted portraits of the lead actors. He even *became* one of the hundreds of actors in the show. Remembering the Cavalcade, Chang says:

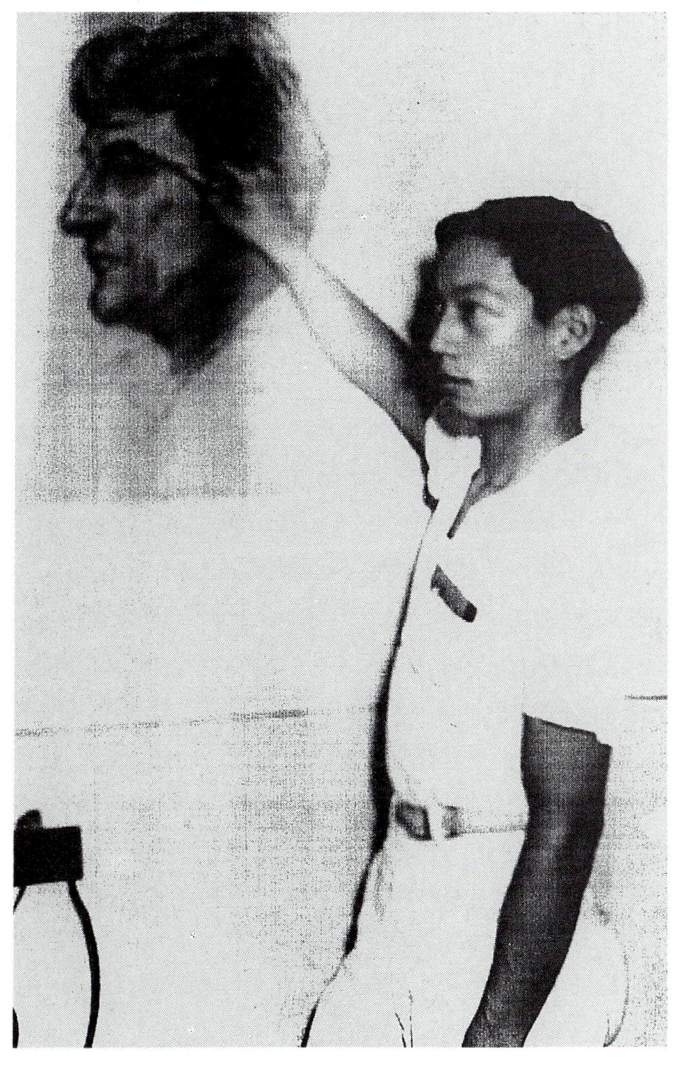

When Wah Chang was eighteen, he made a charcoal sketch of Blanding Sloan.

> The pageant was put on in a big open-air stage . . . big enough for a herd of cattle to go through it, also for four horses [side-by-side] to ride over the ramp in the background. The sets [like the Alamo] were built on railroad flat cars and rolled in.[9]

While working on the *Cavalcade*, Wah Chang was introduced to a young woman who would change his life. Chang met Glennella Taylor on a blind date. Taylor was a seventeen-year-old college student who lived in Denton, thirty-five miles north of Dallas. She had come to work on the *Cavalcade* with many other college students.

"Glen," as her friends called her, was already in her second year of college. She studied education and art. Glen was fascinated by the actors' portraits Wah Chang had painted. She was also fascinated with the artist himself.[10]

When the *Centennial* ended, Chang stayed in Dallas for a year. He and a friend tried to start a business. But because of the Great Depression, there weren't enough customers.

Wah closed the business. He returned to California. Shortly after his return in 1937, Chang heard from his father. Dai Song had just married. He planned a honeymoon trip to China. The first stop would be Wah's birthplace,

At The Texas Centennial, *Wah met seventeen-year-old Glennella Taylor. Glen, who worked as an actress in the production, appears in costume in this photo with Wah and Calvin Sloan, Blanding's son. She and Calvin are wearing their costumes.*

Honolulu, Hawaii. Dai Song wanted Wah to come along on the trip. Wah agreed.[11]

In Honolulu, Chang worked for a short time at a pineapple canning factory. But he found the job boring.[12] And soon after that, he went to work as an art teacher for the Honolulu Recreational Department. Chang gave art lessons to children. He and the children planned an exhibit to show the students' work.

After a year in Hawaii, Wah Chang received a letter from his friend Orville Goldner. Goldner had created special effects for the movie *King Kong*. He wanted Chang to come to work at the *San Francisco World's Fair.* [13]

The World's Fair

Chang arrived in San Francisco in 1938. Plans were being made to hold the *World's Fair* on an island in the bay. Wah Chang helped make some of the exhibits. He created a huge mural. It showed the history of housing from "cave-man to present-day skyscrapers."[14]

Chang also made puppets and sets for the *World's Fair*. And he created three stop-motion animation movies. The *World's Fair* was Chang's

first experience with stop-motion animation. There was no one around to teach Chang, so he taught himself.[15]

When Chang made a stop-motion animation film, he would pose the characters, film them, and stop the film. Next, he would move the characters just the tiniest bit. Then, he would film the characters in the new position and stop the film again. He would do this hundreds or thousands of times, depending on the length of the film. When the film was complete, it would look as though the characters were actually moving.

Within a year, Chang finished his work at the *World's Fair.* By this time, people everywhere were raving about Walt Disney's first full-length animated feature, *Snow White and the Seven Dwarfs*.

The Disney Studio was about to begin work on its second animated film. A friend suggested that Chang come to Hollywood to apply for a job with Disney.[16]

CHALLENGES

In 1939, at twenty-one years old, Wah Chang began work as the youngest member of the Special Effects and Models Department at Walt Disney Studios.[1] The job at Disney was a good one. Chang enjoyed his work. But he earned only $20 per week, one fifth of the salary he had made while working for the *World's Fair.*[2]

Pinocchio

Chang used his experience with puppets for his first Disney project. Disney had decided to make an animated moved based on *The Adventures of*

Pinocchio, an Italian folk tale written by Collodi in 1883.

The animators, artists who drew the cartoons, needed to see how a string puppet moves. They asked for Chang's help.[3] So Chang served as a true-life "Gepetto." He carved his Pinocchio with care.

Chang's work on *Pinocchio* did not stop with the star puppet. He made other puppets. He also made the stagecoach and clocks for the movie. And when viewers were delighted by the sight of the wagon pulled by Pinocchio, they were watching a Wah Chang creation.

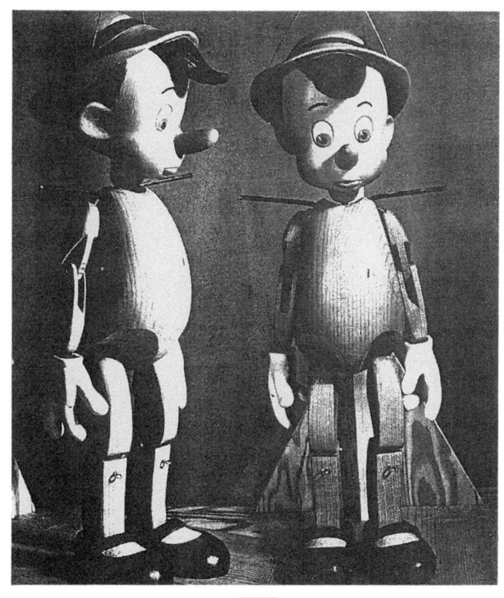

Disney animators gave Chang character model sheets, drawings of Pinocchio. Using the character model sheets, Chang created this Pinocchio puppet. The puppet is shown here from front and side views.

After *Pinocchio*, animators were ready to begin work on *Bambi*. But first, they needed to see just how a

real deer moves.[4] Chang made deer models with movable parts.

After studying Chang's models, animators performed their magic with *Bambi.*

Though Chang is modest about his work with Disney Studios, others are quick to mention the value of his creativity. Many years after Chang left Disney, a director from the Disney Studio would be thrilled to see Wah Chang sculptures in a gallery. He would tell the gallery owner that Chang had been wonderful to work with. Chang always noticed details. He was able to solve work problems for himself and others. When the director could not solve a problem, he would turn to Chang. And Chang could almost always come up with a solution.[5]

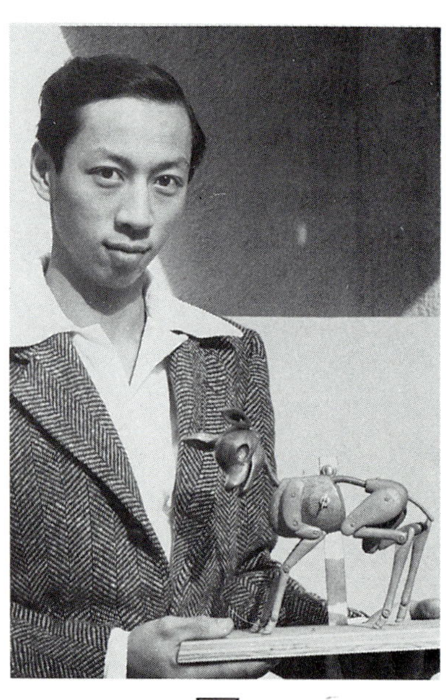

Wah Ming Chang holds a Bambi model he made for Disney animators.

After several

months with Disney, Chang took off across the country on summer vacation. He went to Indiana to pick up a new car he had bought. On the way back to California, he visited Glen Taylor in Texas.[6]

This was the first time the two had seen each other in four years. Glen Taylor says, "I enjoyed renewing our friendship. He still was definitely a very interesting fellow, and great fun to be with. We found a depth of friendship that had not faded with time."[7]

After visiting Glen Taylor, Chang returned to California. He had to get back to his job at Disney Studios.

Panic in the Hospital

Chang had been back from summer vacation for only a short time. He knew he was sick. He hurt all over. He thought he had a bad case of the flu. But Chang's sickness wouldn't go away. It only grew worse. And soon, he found himself in a hospital bed.

A group of doctors came to Chang's bedside. They began examining him. One of them asked, "Can you raise your leg?"[8]

"That's a silly thing to ask!" Chang thought. He tried to raise his leg, something he had been easily able to do for the twenty-one years of his life.[9] But Chang's leg would not move. He was not able to raise it! Wah Ming Chang had given the gift of motion to so many creations. And now, he lay in his hospital bed, unable to move his legs![10]

Polio had struck Wah Ming Chang. No medicine had yet been invented to stop the spread of this feared sickness. It would be the late 1950s before Jonas Salk would develop a vaccine to guard against polio.[11] Until then, the disease would take the lives of thousands and leave thousands of others crippled.

Chang knew very little about polio. But he knew how he felt. He could not move his legs, and he ached all over.[12] Doctors ran many tests. They used a special needle to take fluid out of Chang's spine. The doctors didn't tell Chang what they thought might happen to him. They didn't explain whether he was getting better or getting worse. They didn't even tell him if he would or wouldn't walk again. Still, Wah Chang did not panic—until they wheeled in the iron lung.[13]

The iron lung looked like a long tank raised

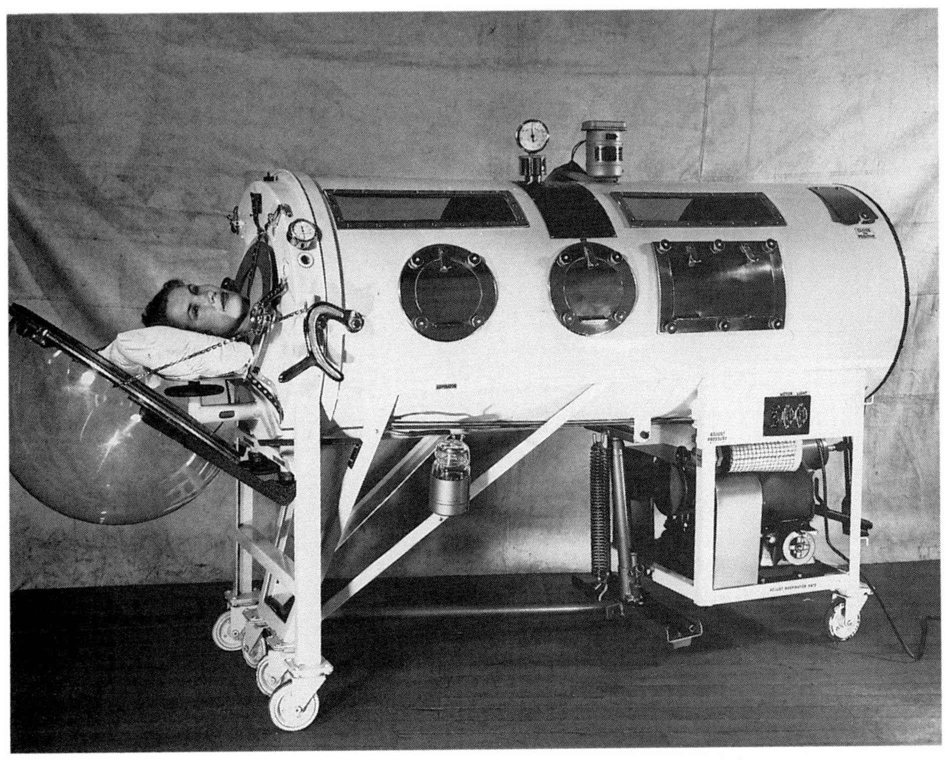

The iron lung kept many polio victims alive by making it possible for them to breathe.

up to bed-level on wheels. Because polio could attack any nerve in the body, it sometimes paralyzed the nerves that sent messages to breathing muscles. When that happened, the polio victim had to be placed in an iron lung to be able to breathe. Chang had heard that once

put in an iron lung, a patient might have to live inside of it forever.[14]

To add to his terror, Chang woke up one night in the hospital hearing frightening sounds across the hall:

> I heard the nurse running down the hall. I could hear her calling for the doctor. A few minutes later, hurried footsteps . . . and the doctor talking and then the sound of the pumping iron lung stopped. There was a lot of noise and bustling about. I knew then that the patient had died.[15]

The terror did not stop.

> In the room next to me I could see activity. The walls were about shoulder high, and from there up, glass. You couldn't hear what was going on, but you could see peoples' heads moving. I knew from the activity going on, that whoever was in that room had also died.[16]

Wah Chang lay ill in his hospital bed. He eyed the iron lung next to him. He waited in fear as the people around him died. Finally, after several days, he had reason to feel some relief.[17]

Chang learned that he would not need the iron lung. He would not even have to stay much longer in the hospital.[18] Instead, Chang could leave the hospital after twenty-one days. He was told that polio could be contagious for that long.

At the end of the twenty-one days, Wah

Chang would leave his hospital bed. He would begin a new and difficult part of his life. Many months of hardship and challenges lay ahead of Wah Ming Chang. He would soon become a patient at a sanitarium. At this special hospital, he would try to learn to walk again.

"No Strings To Hold Me Down"

— *Pinocchio*
Walt Disney Studios

When Wah Chang arrived at the special hospital, he was very weak. Polio had affected the muscles in his legs, back, chest, and arms. He could not walk. He spent his days in bed, or in a wheelchair.[1]

Chang found that he could no longer do many of the simple things he had once taken for granted, like winding his watch. And, for the rest of his life, he would never have enough strength in his lungs to blow up a balloon.[2]

Chang wanted to send a letter to his friend Glen Taylor. He wanted to tell her what had happened. But his hand muscles were not yet

strong enough for him to be able to write. So he asked a nurse to write down his words for Glen.[3]

Glen Taylor remembers the letter well:

> I was deeply shaken by the news. I couldn't imagine that he was almost completely paralyzed! His dictation was that I was not to worry about him, he was already feeling better. But I knew about this disease. After that I wrote to him every few days.[4]

Life at the Hospital

Wah Chang's day began with a bath and a massage. Then nurses would wheel him out to the yard where he would visit with the four or five other patients. They all became good friends. Sometimes, they played practical jokes on one another.[5]

But most of Chang's time was spent playing cards or reading magazines. He quickly grew bored with the routine.[6] One day, Blanding Sloan came to visit. He and Wah Chang came up with a plan.

Sloan returned the next day with a strong, wooden work bench and art supplies. He set up the work bench on a porch. For days, Chang would quietly roll his wheelchair up to the bench and go about the work of creating. It wasn't long

WALT DISNEY

July 20, 1940.

Dear Wah:

It was only a few days ago that I learned of your serious illness, but I am happy to know, through Mr. Keener, that you have passed through the crisis successfully, and that you are now on the road to recovery.

It's a tough seige, I know, but I am sure you have what it takes to put you back on your feet again. We're all pulling for you here and hoping that you'll be back with us soon.

With my kindest regards and every good wish,

Sincerely,

Walt Disney

Mr. Wah Ming Chang,
Twin Oaks Sanitarium,
1302 So. Charlotte Ave.,
San Gabriel, Calif.

WD:DV

Walt Disney sent a get-well message when he learned that Chang had gone to a special hospital to recover from polio.

before other patients began to wheel themselves up beside Chang to ask about his artwork.[7]

Soon, the porch turned into a craft shop. Chang and his friends began making and selling colorful pins. They sold hundreds to hospital visitors. And soon a Los Angeles store began to sell the pins.

Months passed. During the holidays, Chang sat with friends near the Christmas tree. Patients' leg braces hung alongside the decorations.

Day after day, Chang spent long hours doing special exercises to make his muscles stronger. He was finally fitted for leg braces, and given crutches. Wah Ming Chang was learning how to walk all over again.

After a long year, Chang left the hospital to go home. He returned to live with Blanding Sloan and Mildred Taylor. Soon, Chang needed only his leg braces. He threw away his crutches. He was able to walk again![8] Polio had not beaten Wah Ming Chang.

Love and Marriage

Wah Chang had beaten polio and Glen Taylor was inspired. She wrote, "Learning how a fellow

human can summon the strength and the will to cope with life so suddenly and drastically altered, and to do it cheerfully, taught me to appreciate life's wonderful possibilities."[9]

Glen Taylor spent the summer of 1941 visiting relatives in California. She and Wah dated often. Before the end of August, they were engaged. Chang comments, "Glen says she proposed to me, but I'm not sure who proposed to whom. Every year, we joke about it these days, as to who was the one that did the proposing."[10]

At the end of the summer, Glen Taylor had to return to her teaching job in Austin, Texas. On the way, she stopped in Denton to break the news of the engagement to her parents. Her parents were *very* upset. They did not want their daughter to marry Wah Chang.[11]

Glen says:

> I made several trips home, each one a . . . battle between two parents who loved me deeply and wanted to save me from the disaster I was planning, and my own certainty that there would be no other man in my life but this one, and that we would be able to cope with whatever lay ahead as long as we had each other.[12]

Glen Taylor and Wah Chang were in love. Nothing could change that. The two *would* be

married. It was just a question of when and where.

On December 7, 1941, the Japanese bombed Pearl Harbor, and the United States entered World War II. The war created many hardships.

Glen and Wah lived far from each other when the war broke out. Glen lived in Texas, and Wah lived in California. Travel was difficult. It was hard to get airline tickets. And driving presented problems of its own. Gasoline was rationed. Most of the gasoline went to soldiers who were fighting the war. And at home in America, drivers were allowed only very small amounts of gas. As the war went on, travel problems grew worse across the country.[13]

Wah and Glen decided that it would be wise to meet and marry right away.[14]

Should Glen travel to California or should Wah travel to Texas? The two did not have a chance to make the decision themselves. California law had already done that for them. It was against the law for a Caucasian and a Chinese to be married in California.[15]

So, Wah Chang traveled to Texas in March of 1942 for the wedding. Ironically, if Wah had been African American, he and Glen could not

have been married in Texas. There, marriage between a Caucasian and an African American was illegal in 1942.[16]

After their marriage, the newlyweds went to see Glen's parents. Still unhappy with their daughter's decision, the Taylors had not come to the wedding. Chang remembers, "I must say while they inwardly did not accept this marriage, they were more than kind to me while I was there."[17]

In years to come, Glen's parents would accept Wah Chang fully. In fact, Glen's widowed father would even come to live with the Changs during the last years of his life. [18]

Wah and Glen Chang drove back to California after their wedding. There they lived for a short time in a tent in the Sloan/Taylor's backyard. Soon, they moved into their own apartment.[19]

Wah worked for George Pal's Studio and then for John Sutherland's Studio. He made short, animated puppet films. He also made training films for the Army and Navy. Glen went to work for the Air Force handing out supplies to soldiers.

By 1945, Wah and Glen Chang were ready to use their many skills to create their own films. The two invested $1500, their life savings, in

Wah and Glen Chang joke with each other as they prepare to leave for California after their Texas wedding.

camera equipment. They set out to start a new film company.[20]

The Changs worked together to make a number of films. One showed a treatment to help polio victims. Others were educational films and were used in schools.

Sloan and Chang Together Again

It had been some time since Wah Chang had worked with Blanding Sloan. But now, a special project came their way. In 1946, Lutheran minister Hubert Rasbach asked Sloan and Chang to make a puppet film about the Atomic Age.[21]

World War II had ended in 1945 with the atomic bombing of Hiroshima. People all over the world were thinking about the dangers in a world with atomic bombs.

Some years later, in classrooms across America, students would do the "duck and cover" drill. They would practice hiding under their desks and covering their heads—in case of an atomic attack. Fear of "the bomb" had come to America.

Wah and Glen Chang worried about the world's future.[22]

The Way of Peace

Wah and Glen Chang were invited to Washington, D.C., in 1947. The occasion was a celebration of a Sloan/Chang film. President Harry S. Truman and Albert Einstein had also been invited to be part of this history-making event.[1]

The time arrived. As people sat waiting, they were surrounded by darkness. Sounds blared from a loudspeaker. Then, it came. Men ran quickly about. They pulled atomic bombs from hidden caves. The bombs sailed through the air. Explosions rang out. Smoke rose to the sky. And then, it was over. Pieces of homes sat in piles. Smoking hills rose up where factories had stood.

Lifeless bodies lay everywhere. A fiery smoking ball, once known as the earth, burned—until the planet disintegrated.

Stillness filled the air.

Then applause rang out. The audience clapped for *The Way of Peace*, a film produced by Wah Chang and Blanding Sloan.[2] The film showed the history of the earth, from its beginning to an atomic end. No human actors appeared in the movie. All of the film's characters were made of metal and rubber. And a new type of stop-action photography was used.

Film Drama of Atomic Bomb Premiere to Be Held Tonight

Blanding Sloan (left) and Mr. and Mrs. Wah Ming Chang who are in Washington for the showing tonight in Constitution Hall of "The Way of Peace." —Star Staff Photo

Wah and Glen Chang, along with Blanding Sloan, made headlines in Washington, D.C. when The Way of Peace *was shown in Constitution Hall.*

A magazine article praised the photography,

the miniature settings, and the use of models and puppets.[3]

Today, Lutheran Minister Rasbach says, "He [Wah Chang] had a great love for humanity . . . the work was just excellent. He was able to produce the reality I was seeking."[4]

The Gorilla

After *The Way of Peace*, work slowed down for Chang and Sloan. Chang did some work on his own. Then, he formed a company with his friend Gene Warren. Chang and Warren had worked together in the past.

Today, Warren says he has always thought of his friend Wah Chang as a genius. He speaks of how happy he was working with Chang. "He's one of the most wonderful people I've known in my life."[5]

Chang and Warren handled hundreds of projects. They made props for theater companies. They created award-winning commercials. And they provided costumes and special effects for television shows and movies.

Chang made many costumes for famous actors and actresses. One of them was the

realistic gorilla suit he produced in the 1940s. Because the actor scheduled to wear the suit had a heart attack, he was unable to use the costume right away. So the Changs kept the costume in their home. The gorilla sat on their living room sofa for weeks. Once it even sat on their toilet and frightened a party guest.[6]

During the 1960s, Chang's projects included a headdress for Shirley MacLaine in the movie Can Can.

Toys and Tarantulas

Chang made masks for the ballet sequence in The King and I.

One of the Chang's projects involved a famous young woman less than a foot tall. Her name was "Barbie."™ Though Chang says he didn't design the final product, he worked on a model for the doll known by children all over the world today.[7]

Chang also designed many other kinds of toys. One toy was made by using a bent wire inside a rubber animal. The rubber animal sat on a plastic, round base. Turning the crank on the bottom of the base made the animal move. Children loved these toys. Stores wanted more! Chang's company had eighty people working day and night to assemble and ship the animal toys all over the United States![8]

While people worked on toys in one part of the factory, it was not at all unusual for Wah Chang and Gene Warren to be working on a science-fiction film in another. This was usually not a problem. But, on one film, the actors got a little bit out of hand.

The problem came up while Chang and Warren were working on a movie about tarantulas. For the film, they created several huge fake tarantulas. Each had a leg span of about six feet, and looked very real. Chang and Warren also decided to use forty *live* tarantulas. They put these hairy creatures near very tiny model buildings. Then they added tiny helicopters. This made the tarantulas look really huge. Chang explains:

> All this took place in our toy factory. There were the toy assembly workers working on the toys, and during their breaks they passed through the part of the building where we were shooting the tarantula scenes. When we got through . . . and the movie crew started collecting the live tarantulas, we found that one or two were missing and unaccounted for. Well, for weeks after that, our crew was very uneasy, and kept a sharp lookout for the stray actors. We never did find them.[9]

After the tarantula movie, the toy company continued to enjoy very good business. Chang decided to try to give sound to his moving animal toys. His company spent thousands of dollars, but the sound just never seemed to work quite right. The company stopped making toys in 1948.

Wah Chang receives a surprise visit from one of the giant tarantulas he created for a movie.

In 1956, Chang and Warren began a new company. The name of the company, "Project Unlimited," could only begin to predict the Chang and Warren creations of the future.

"And the Oscar Goes To . . ."

On any given day, visitors to Project Unlimited Studio might find themselves face-to-face with dinosaurs, ghosts, two-headed monsters, dragons, skeletons, and any number of other creations.

Author and English professor Dr. David Barrow is Glen Chang's cousin. He remembers well a visit to Project Unlimited when he was only five years old. He says:

> . . . my parents took our family to visit Wah Chang's studio in California where we were introduced to Wah's latest creations: manipulable [movable], foot-high dinosaurs, so real that my younger brother and I were at first afraid to

> venture too close, afraid that we'd be bitten. But soon Wah had coaxed us nearer, explaining how the monsters were made and patiently demonstrating some technique or another he used in bringing the dinosaurs to life. One of them [the dinosaurs] missed a patch of skin on its flank, and there was exposed the delicate arrangement of wires and metal joints beneath the artists' illusion—a powerful revelation for a five-year-old. I have carefully keep this image over the years, of the partially flayed [stripped] creation and, standing behind it, Wah Chang, gentle, quiet, his hands tucked modestly in his pockets . . . .[1]

Barrow also remembers Chang's attitude toward children. "Children seem to know when they are being taken seriously, and it seems to me now that . . . what I thought of those creatures mattered very much to Wah."[2]

During the Project Unlimited years, Chang would produce special effects, masks, props, and animation that would become some of his best-known work.[3]

The Time Machine

The Time Machine would become one of Chang's most famous films. Project Unlimited would win two Academy Awards for the film's special effects.[4]

Chang built the miniature model of the time

Pictured here, from left to right: Tim Baar, Wah Chang, George Pal, and Gene Warren proudly display an academy award for special effects in The Time Machine.

machine. His company also created many of the special effects that made the movie believable.

Many scenes in the film took place inside the time machine. A magazine article explained that the film would have been lost without the special effects that showed the art of time travel.

The article described some of the astounding effects in the film:

> They [Wah Chang and Gene Warren] show time passing in a number of ways: the sun zips across the skylight, a snail races across the ground, flowers open and shut like umbrellas, and the fashionable dresses on a mannequin in the window of a clothing store change styles as the seasons and the years pass.[5]

Wah Chang works behind the camera during the filming of The Time Machine.

One of the special effects Chang and Warren created for *The Time Machine* was a volcanic eruption. When the time came to show the lava blazing through a town, Chang's creative genius once again sprang into action. He and partner Gene Warren decided to use oatmeal, colored with red dye, to be photographed under special red lights.[6] But how to force this make-believe lava to race through the town?

First, the town was built with miniature props that matched the full-size town in the movie. The buildings and streets were built on tilted ramps, so the lava could flow smoothly and easily. Chang and Warren decided to use giant containers above the sound stage to hold the lava. When the time was right, the doors to the containers would be opened, and the oatmeal would spill into the town.

The scene was to be filmed on a Monday. Two-hundred-fifty gallons of oatmeal were cooked up in preparation on the Friday before. The cooked oatmeal was then poured into the containers, and the containers were sealed. On Monday, Chang and Warren began filming the volcano scene in a small room. The two stood practically against the wall behind their high-speed cameras. They gave the signal: "Let'er go!"[7]

Watery red oatmeal raced out of the containers through the tiny town. A terrible odor filled the room. The oatmeal had spoiled over the weekend. It smelled awful! What was worse, it no longer looked like lava. It didn't even look

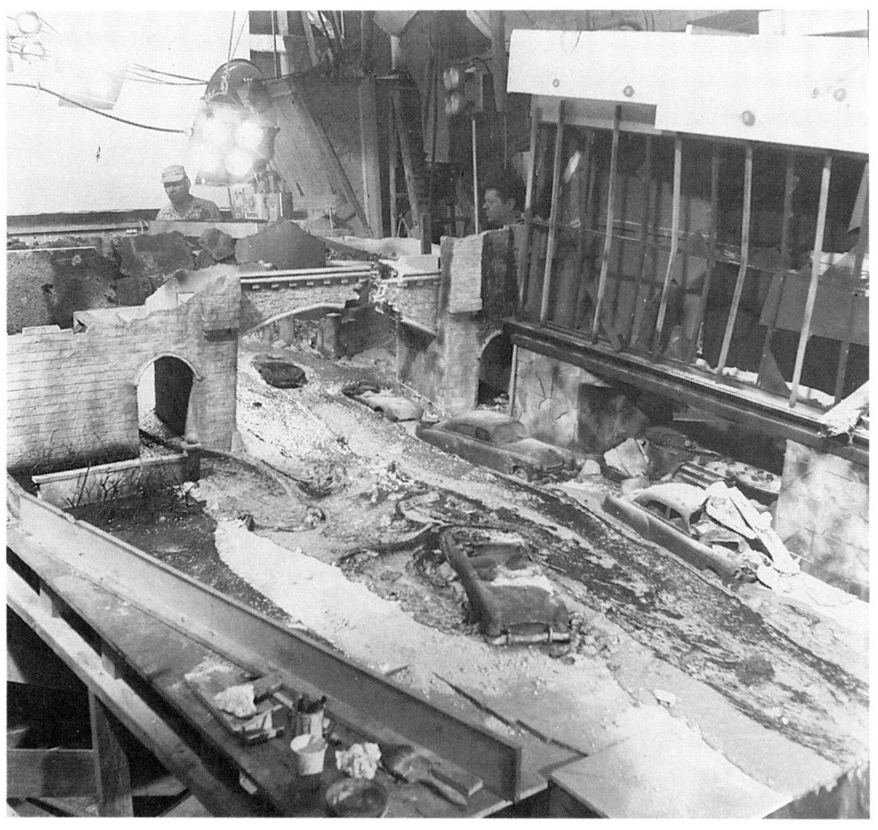

A miniature set from The Time Machine *shows the town after a volcanic eruption.*

like oatmeal. After rotting, it simply ran through the town like red water. Chang and Warren were trapped behind their cameras. The room was so small, they had nowhere to run. The red mess raced toward them. Stinking, watery, red oatmeal pinned them to the wall.

Still, all was not lost. At least Chang and Warren had thought to cover the mini-town with plastic for the filming.[8] Under the plastic, the town was clean and ready to face another

Chang made this model of the time machine for the movie.

volcanic blast. The next time Chang and Warren filmed the scene, they used *fresh* oatmeal. And when people all over the world watched *The Time Machine*, they saw a frightening, realistic volcanic explosion.

Monsters and Spaceships

Chang's puppets and special effects brought to life many films and commercials of the 1950s and 1960s. When television viewers watched the broad smiles and giggles of the Pillsbury Dough Boy,™ they saw a face that had come from the hands of Wah Chang.

Other Wah Chang projects from this time included props for *Planet of the Apes* and scary skeleton animation for *The Power*. In *The Power,* a head was shown losing its skin, losing its muscle, and ending up as nothing more than bones.

Chang designed and made many frightening monsters and special effects for a popular 1960s television show. *Outer Limits* featured a different monster each week.

The monsters for *Outer Limits* had to be created on very short notice. So, Chang and Warren went to the earliest script meetings. The

two made suggestions, and Chang actually began to sketch the monsters before leaving.[9]

In the *Outer Limits* episode "The Architects of Fear," Chang's creature was considered so horrifying that it was never shown on the screen from head to toe at one time. Instead, viewers saw only a bit of an arm or a shot of the legs. Even so, some networks took out the scenes with the monster. Others showed "The Architects of Fear" episode very late at night.[10]

Chang not only created the terrifying creatures for *Outer Limits*; he often worked behind the camera. He and Warren filmed many special effects, including spaceships, rays, disintegrations, warps, and shimmers.

Helping Others

Even with their busy schedules, Chang and Warren took time for the people who worked for them. The two looked for projects that would help the careers of the special effects artists who worked for them.[11]

Some of these special-effects artists had already done well-known work. Others would go on to become part of behind-the-scenes crews in

famous television shows and movies. Marcel Delgado had worked with Willis O'Brien on the movie *King Kong*. Don Sahlin would later join the crew of Muppet-creator Jim Henson. Bob Mattey would go on to create the mechanical killer shark in *Jaws*.[12]

By 1966, Chang was beginning a new mission. His creative journey would take him to a new frontier. He would boldly go where no one had gone before.™

"To Boldly Go Where No One Has Gone Before"™

— *Star Trek*
Paramount Studios

On September 8, 1966, an American legend was born. Television viewers watched the first episode of *Star Trek.* The show was not a great success in its own time, but it did become very popular after it went off the air. In its honor, conventions are held all over the world today.

Wah Chang had a hand in *Star Trek's* earliest creations. *Outer Limits* and *Star Trek* producer Robert H. Justman says, "Wah's work was always of the highest quality and very high creativity, and certainly he made it possible for us to do what we were doing on *Star Trek.* He made our jobs possible."[1]

Phasers and Communicators

Star Trek creator Gene Rodenberry and producer Robert Justman knew they would need special props for *Star Trek*. The show's characters would use phaser pistols, tricorders, and communicators.[2]

Others had tried to make a phaser pistol model for the show, but they had not done a good job. Justman wanted Chang to make the model he needed.

Chang took the drawings of the phaser. He agreed to return with a completed model. He also agreed to design and create the tricorder and the communicator. Justman says that Wah Chang finished everything "perfectly."[3]

Chang had a creative, successful association with *Star Trek*. His many *Star Trek* creatures have become famous.

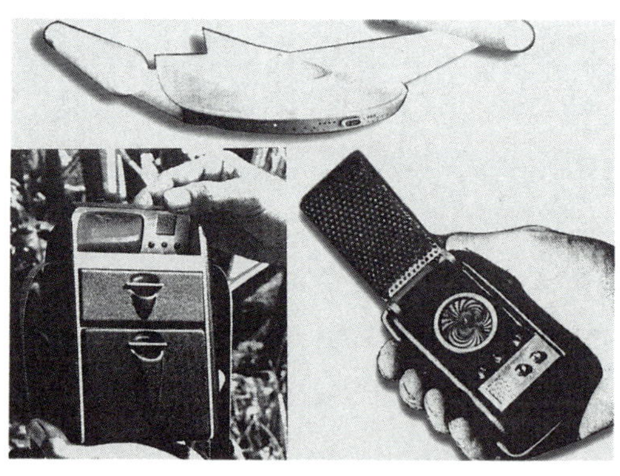

Chang worked successfully for Star Trek *for many years. Among his creations were the tricorder, the communicator, and a Romulan space vessel.*

Chang created the Balock effigy for "The

Corbomite Maneuver" episode. This frightening character quickly became the background for the credits after each *Star Trek* episode.

For the "Mantrap" episode of *Star Trek*, Chang created the salt-sucking monster, also known as the salt vampire. In this episode, a beautiful woman turns into a hideous monster. It has octopus-like suction cups all over its long

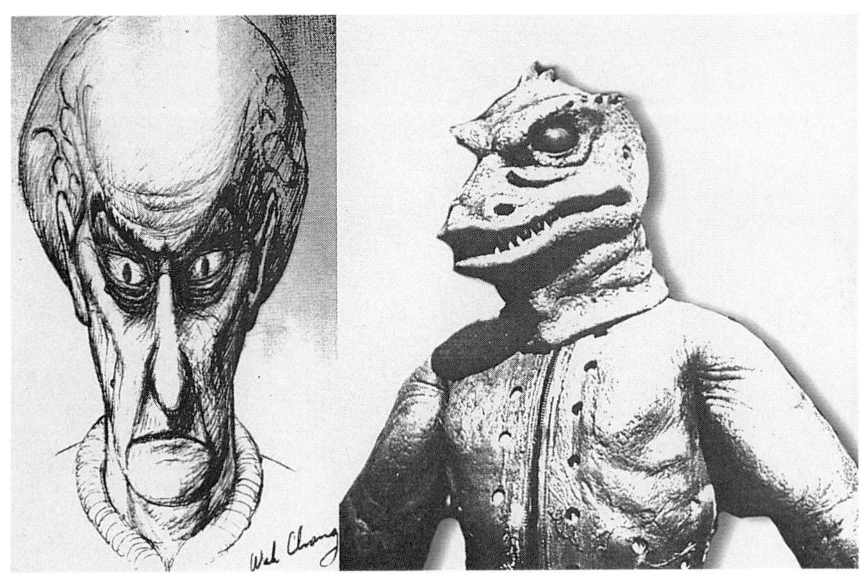

Among the monsters Chang created for Star Trek *were the Gorn from the "Arena" episode (right) and the Balock effigy, which appeared as the background for the credits at the end of the show.*

fingertips. The monster uses the suction cups to suck all of the salt from its live victims.

Another of Chang's popular *Star Trek* monsters is the Gorn. In the "Arena" episode, Captain Kirk is transported to the Gorn's planet. He and the Gorn begin to battle. The creature's strength is far superior to that of the captain. So Kirk must use his wits, rather than his fists, to win the battle. For the Gorn, Chang created a rubber mask. The costume was worn over a diver's wet suit.

Chang also created the Neanderthal man for "The Galileo Seven," and a Romulan space vessel used in "Balance of Terror."

The furry, likable tribbles from "The Trouble with Tribbles" became a popular favorite. Chang created the tribbles by using artificial fur stuffed with foam.

About Wah Chang, producer Robert Justman says, "He's a very fine human being. Certainly he's a creatively fine sculptor. He's a wonderful artist and a lovely person, and he never, ever disappointed us with *Star Trek* or *Outer Limits*. I have nothing but high regard for him."[4]

By the late 1960s, fewer fantasy and science-fiction films were being made. Chang and Warren decided to close Project Unlimited. After

closing the business, they held an auction at the studio to raise money.[5] Advertisements for the auction appeared in monster magazines all over the country.

The day of the auction arrived. People came from everywhere. They were "bidding like crazy."[6] The crowd was hungry for more. Chang and Warren dashed back to the trash bins. They started pulling out anything they thought might be of value. Chang says, "they snapped these up as precious treasures, the old ragged worn out puppets, in pieces, some of them, that we had cleaned out and discarded."[7]

Shortly after closing Project Unlimited, Chang and Warren decided to open up a new studio. They created a number of costumes for *Ice Capades* and the *Ice Follies*. They also made many television commercials.

A New Life

By the end of 1970, Wah and Glen Chang tired of the long drive to Hollywood from their Altadena home. They wanted to get away from the traffic, the smog, and the "pressure of the work with long hours, short deadlines, and small budgets."[8] It was time for a drastic change in lifestyle.

The Changs left Altadena, where they had lived for twenty-five years. They moved to Carmel Valley, California.

Wah Chang designed and built their home himself.[9] The house was built right into a hillside. Windows across the back of the house looked out onto the green valley. Trees blanketed the hill. Birds often came to the porch to sing.

In the Changs' hall, Sloan's portrait of Wah in his cowboy suit hung on the wall. Framed sketches of *Star Trek* props hung nearby. Pictures of the Changs with other famous people from Hollywood also lined the walls.

Down the hall and around the corner, stairs led down to Wah Chang's art studio.

Friends of the Environment

Wah Chang's art studio would soon become filled with his sculptures of wildlife. Even before moving to Carmel, the Changs had become very interested in the environment. They were concerned about issues such as overpopulation and endangered wildlife. The two had joined the Sierra Club. And, they had decided to work on environmental and educational films.[10] The Changs produced *Dinosaurs,*

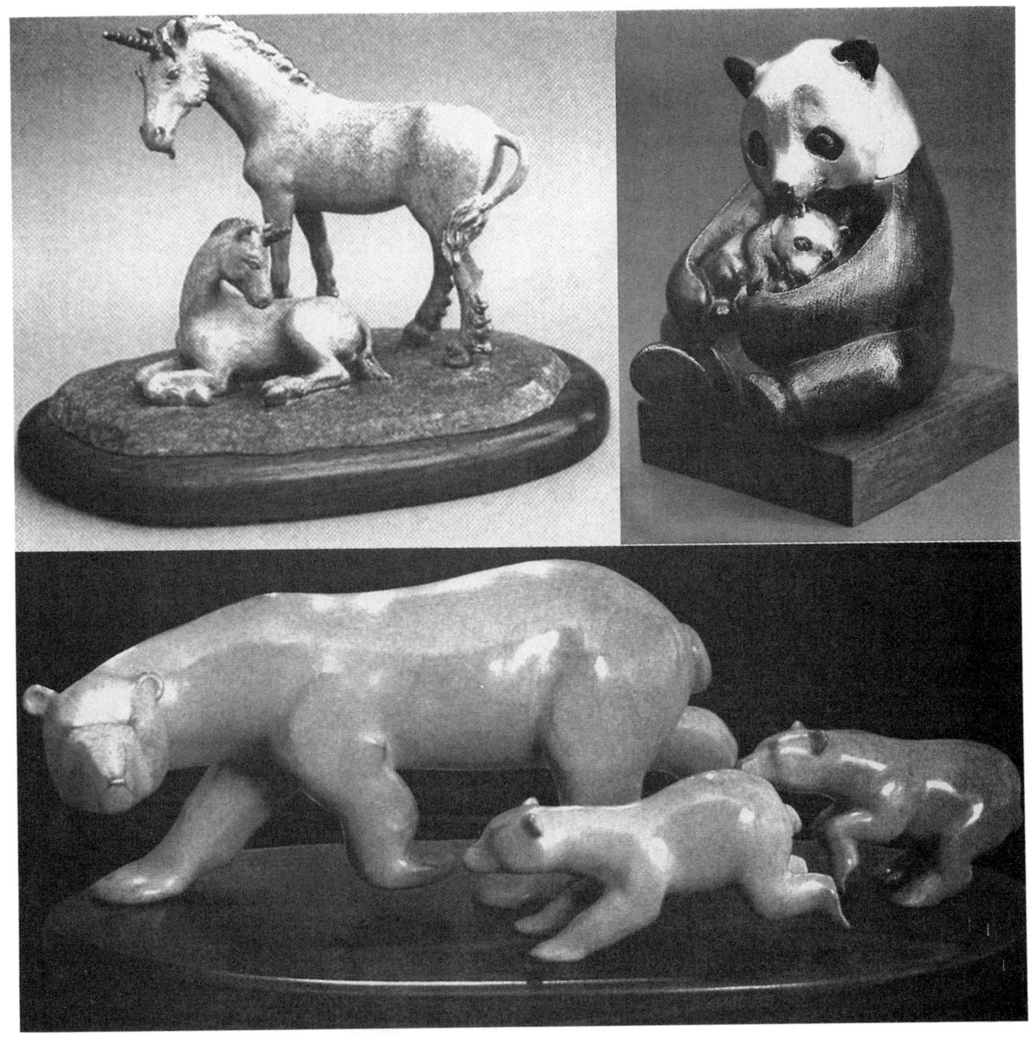

Wildlife is a primary theme in much of Chang's artwork. His hundreds of sculptures include: "Unicorns," "Panda," and "Running Polar Bears."

The Terrible Lizards, and *Man's Effect on the Environment*.

After the move to Carmel Valley, they took a long trip through the western states and shot footage for an endangered-wildlife film, *Ecology*—Wanted Alive. The film won an award.[11]

The idea for a film on sea otters was born when the Changs met attorney Bill Bryan. He had done a great deal of underwater filming. Bryan asked Wah Chang to edit the thousands of feet of film. Chang agreed.[12] He combined Bryan's film with film he had taken himself. The result was *Otters, Clowns of the Sea*.

The film showed what delightful mammals sea otters are. It also looked at their problems. Sea otters had become endangered. Thousands of people were killing them for their thick fur coats.

Wah and Glen Chang saw the problems of the sea otter and of so many other creatures. The two had an important goal in their lives. They wanted to work toward solutions of environmental problems.[13]

The Creative Journey Is Never Complete

Though Wah Chang worked for the environment after moving to Carmel, he had not given up all of his ties to Hollywood.[1] The artist might be focusing on wildlife sculptures one moment and making a puppet for a television show the next.[2]

As Chang worked in Carmel, he remained close to Blanding Sloan. But, in 1975, Chang lost the man who had taught him the art of puppetry—and so much more. Chang would miss Sloan, the man who had discovered and encouraged a young boy's talent.[3] But Chang still

had Mildred Taylor. He would keep in touch with her until her death in the early 1990s.

Dennis the Menace™

More and more, Wah Chang worked with his sculpting. He sculpted first in plastic, and then in bronze. The artist created his bronze sculptures by using the lost wax process, a four-thousand-year-old Chinese method of casting metal.[4]

Chang sent many of his sculptures to nearby galleries. He found that his work sold quite well.

In 1987, Dennis the Menace™ creator Hank Ketcham contacted Chang. Ketcham had doodled some sketches and thought about how "neat" it would be to have Dennis as a 3-D(three-dimensional) member of the family.[5]

Ketcham took his sketches to Wah Chang. Chang immediately set about the business of creating the statue. When he finished the work, Ketcham was very pleased. "I was delighted to see the little boy in 3-D."[6]

Ketcham had four identical statues made from Chang's sculpting. He put one Dennis statue in his garden. He put another in his studio and another at the Arnold Palmer Children's

Hospital. The fourth statue found a home in Dennis Park in Monterey, California, very close to the Changs' home.

The 1987 unveiling of the statue at Dennis Park was an important event. The mayor, the park commissioners, and hundreds of children and parents came to see the charming statue.[7]

Ketcham remembers Wah Chang's reaction that day at the park.

> . . . you could see little smiles and laughter all over his eyes. He was very glad on the outside . . . he seemed to enjoy the association and I was certainly proud to have his talent added to the Dennis story. I am sorry that I came along so late in his life that I didn't get a chance to share other things with him, but I feel privileged to have met him at that time.[8]

Hank Ketcham, the creator of Dennis the Menace,™ asked Chang to create a life-size sculpture of the famous character.

Wah Chang has been delighted to visit the statue in the park over the years.

He says, "The bronze, three-foot 'Dennis' is set on a small elevated bridge which the kids can readily reach and climb on. His nose—and any other handy bump—is well polished by now by the many small hands of neighborhood kids at the playground."[9]

As Chang's work continued with his sculptures, they grew very popular. He began to place them in art galleries all over the country.

A Serious Setback

In 1992, Wah Chang experienced a setback with his health. He was having a problem related to the polio that had attacked him five decades before.

Chang had thrown away his crutches. For over fifty years, he had needed only leg braces to be able to walk. But in 1992, he was struck with post-polio syndrome.

After his fight with polio in 1941, Chang had lost the use of many muscles. This meant that other muscles had to work harder to make up for those that could no longer do their jobs. As a result, Chang began to grow tired very easily. The doctor hold him that he must now use a large metal

walker for support. This was very hard for Chang, but it did not stop him from creating.[10]

By 1995, Wah Chang was still busy in the studio of his Carmel home. He continued to create sculptures that showed his sense of humor, his respect for children, and his concern for the environment. His wife, Glen, had begun to take care of many important matters relating to the sale of the sculptures.

Chang shows his sculpture "Hawk—Tomorrow's Bright Promise."

Wah Chang has created hundreds of sculptures. They reflect his wide variety of experiences. Wildlife is still a primary theme. His sculptures include: "Eagle," "Standing Doe and Fawn," "Baby Seal," "Sea Otter with Pup II," and "Hawk—Tomorrow's Bright Promise."

"Baby Seal," "Standing Doe and Fawn," and "Elephants" illustrate Chang's interest in wildlife.

Inspiring Others

One of the galleries offering the work of Wah Ming Chang is Gary Lawrence's Lawrence Gallery, in Oregon. Lawrence sells the work of over one-hundred-eighty well-known artists. Chang's work is among the top sellers.[11]

When Lawrence, a sculptor himself, talks about the popularity of Chang's work, he says, "The spirit that he puts into each one

Art gallery owner Gary Lawrence says that "Horse II" is a combination of Chang's Oriental heritage and his Disney experience.

of his individual pieces is what makes them special."[12]

Lawrence describes "Horse II," one of Wah's horse sculptures in this way: "Chang's horse is a combination of Chang's Disney experience and his Oriental heritage. That's what makes it so unique. It evokes [brings out] an emotion from you."[13]

When comparing Chang to the great artists of yesteryear, gallery-owner Lawrence says, ". . . the spirit that [Auguste] Rodin [a famous sculptor from the nineteenth century] puts in his work is the same kind of spirit that Wah is able to capture in the pieces that he does."[14]

Lawrence keeps some of Chang's sculptures on the desk in the gallery. Children often are drawn to them. "Children just love to touch it [the sculpture] and look at it and hold it and they are experiencing, learning about art. . . . I've had many children leave in tears because Mom and Dad won't buy them a Wah Chang sculpture."[15]

When speaking about Chang, Lawrence says, "It's always a wonder and a privilege to talk to him . . . He's one wonderful example of what I hope to be."[16]

Lawrence also says that it is typical of Chang to go out of his way to help young artists who are "coming up."[17]

A Legacy

When Wah Chang was only seven years old, he said, "I just have to draw. If I see something

Children often want to touch Chang sculptures, such as "The Last Dragon."

beautiful, I want to put it down—otherwise I become very sad."[18]

For almost eight decades, Wah Chang's joy has come from creating and sharing works of beauty. No hardship during his artistic journey could hold him back.

Wah Ming Chang—etcher, painter, puppeteer, costumer, creator of special effects, filmmaker, and sculptor—has made his artistic voyage with

great talent, keen intelligence, and a delightful sense of humor. He has taken countless others on fantastic journeys of their own, through his astounding creations.

As surely as a smile creeps across the face of a child who touches a Wah Chang sculpture—

as surely as millions delight in the fright from a Wah Chang monster—

as surely as a soul is touched by the plight of wildlife through a Wah Chang film—

as surely as a child is inspired to know the ability to do great things—

as surely as the Carmel hills glow in the oranges and reds of the California sunset . . .

So, surely, will the beauty given to the world by the quiet genius, Wah Ming Chang, live on forever.

CHRONOLOGY

1917—Wah Chang is born on August 2 in Honolulu, Hawaii.

1919—Chang moves to San Francisco, California, with his parents, Fai Sue and Dai Song Chang. They open the Ho Ho Tea Room.

1926—Chang has first one-man art exhibition.

1927—Chang sells his first etching, *Stub—The Dog That Wants to Play*.

1928—Chang's mother dies. He goes to live in the home of Blanding Sloan and Mildred Taylor.

1931—Chang's mural is allowed to remain on the wall at the Peninsula School.

1933—At sixteen, Chang creates sets for *Victory Ball Ballet*.

1937—Chang paints actors' portraits and takes several roles in the *Cavalcade* at *The Texas Centennial*. He meets his future wife, Glenella Taylor, on a blind date.

1938—Chang teaches children in Honolulu, Hawaii, and returns to California to do exhibits and stop-action films for *The World's Fair* in San Francisco.

1939—Chang takes a position at Walt Disney Studios as the youngest member of the Special Effects and Models Department. He carves a model for *Pinocchio*, makes articulated models for *Bambi*, and works on *Fantasia, The Rite of Spring*, and *The Ghost of Bear Mountain*.

1940—Chang is stricken with polio. He goes to the Twin Oaks Sanitarium in San Gabriel, California, to recover.

1941—Chang leaves the sanitarium and becomes engaged to Glen Taylor. He works for George Pal doing Puppetoons as well as other projects.

1942—Wah Ming Chang marries Glen Taylor.

1942–1944—The Changs move to Altadena. Wah works for George Pal, and then for John Sutherland, doing short animated puppet films and making training films for the Army and Navy.

1945—The Changs make educational and medical films.

1946—Chang opens East-West Studios. With

Blanding Sloan, he produces the acclaimed film, *The Way of Peace*.

1947–1956—Wah Ming Chang and Gene Warren go into business. They produce crank toys and a bendable animal. Chang works on the model of the first Barbie™ doll. Chang and Warren make commercials for Bulova™ and others. Chang makes masks for the ballet sequence in *The King and I*; he creates the head for the Pillsbury™ doughboy.

1957–1968—Chang and Warren form Project Unlimited. Project Unlimited wins two academy awards for *The Time Machine* and one academy award for *Tom Thumb*. Other films for which Chang and Warren create puppets and special effects during this time include: *Mutiny on the Bounty, Spartacus, The Seven Faces of Dr. Lao, Dinosauraus, Atlantis: The Lost Continent, Goliath and the Dragon, The Four Horsemen of the Apocalypse, Master of the World, The Wonderful World of the Brothers Grimm, Around the World and Under the Sea*, and *The Power*. Chang creates a headdress for Shirley McLaine in *Can Can*. He creates a headdress for Elizabeth Taylor in the title role of *Cleopatra*. Taylor is featured on the cover of *Life* magazine wearing the headdress.

1963-1965—Chang creates special effects and monsters for the television show *Outer Limits*.

1966—Chang begins his association with *Star Trek*. He makes the phaser pistol with designs from *Star Trek*. He designs and creates the tricorder and the communicator as well as a Romulan space vessel for "Balance of Terror." His *Star Trek* monsters include the Balock effigy from "The Corbomite Maneuver"—this face is eventually used for the background of the credits. Chang also creates the Salt Vampire for "Mantrap," the Gorn for "Arena," the Neanderthal man for "The Galileo Seven," and the tribbles for "The Trouble with Tribbles."

1969—Chang and Warren form Excelsior Studios where they make commercials for Mattel Toy Company,™ McDonald's™ restaurant, Total™ cereal, Barbie,™ and others. The company also does educational films. Chang and Warren create a simulator film for NASA. The film is used by the Apollo astronauts to train for their moon walk mission. Chang creates props for *Planet of the Apes*. He and Warren produce costumes for *Ice Follies* and *Ice Capades*.

1970–1987—The Changs move to Carmel, California where they join the Sierra Club and create educational and environmental films. They win an award for *Ecology—Wanted Alive*; Wah Chang creates dinosaur puppets for Marty and Sid Kroft's Saturday morning show, *Land of the Lost*; Chang begins to concentrate on his sculptures, which are placed in art galleries all over the world; Chang is accepted for membership in the Carmel Art Association, where he serves several terms on the board of directors.

1987—Chang creates Dennis the Menace™ statues at the request of Hank Ketcham.

1987–present—Chang continues to sculpt in his Carmel home. On March 25, 1995, Wah and Glen Chang celebrate their fifty-third wedding anniversary.

Films Including Wah Ming Chang's Creations

*Dates listed are original release dates

Around the World Under the Sea. MGM/UA, 1965

Atlantis: the Lost Continent. MGM/UA, 1961.

Bambi. Walt Disney Video, 1942.

Can Can. Fox Video, 1960.

Cleopatra. Fox Video, 1963.

Dinosaurs. New World Video, 1960.

Fantasia. Walt Disney Video, 1940.

The Four Horsemen of the Apocalypse. MGM/UA, 1961.

Goliath and the Dragon. Sinister Cinema, 1960.

The King and I. Fox Video, 1956.

Master of the World. Orion, 1961.

Mutiny on the Bounty. MGM/UA, 1962.

Pinocchio. Walt Disney Video, 1942.

Planet of the Apes. Fox Video, 1967.

Spartacus. MCA/Universal Home Video, 1960.

The Seven Faces of Dr. Lao. Fox Video, 1963.

The Time Machine. MGM/UA, 1960.

Tom Thumb. MGM/UA, 1958.

The Wonderful World of the Brothers Grimm. MGM/UA, 1962.

Chapter Notes

**Note: For all sources on information listed as "unknown" the information came from Wah Ming Chang's own personal collection of newspaper clippings, which do not include complete references.*

Chapter 1

1. "Wah Ming Chang Hailed as Genius With Brush; Has Exhibited in Leading United States Cities," newspaper and date unknown.
2. "Chinese Boy, 11, Conducts Dry Campaign on Canvas," newspaper and date unknown.

Chapter 2

1. "Chinese Youngster at Age of Eight Puts Name High in Ranks of Child Artists," newspaper unknown, June, 1926.
2. Ibid.
3. David Barrow and Glen Chang, *The Life and Sculpture of Wah Ming Chang* (San Francisco: Sung in Printing, 1989), p. 3.; "East Meets West When Chinese Girl Joins White Actors in Oriental Play," *The San Francisco Call and Post*, date unknown.
4. David Barrow, *The Story of Wah Ming Chang*, unpublished manuscript, date unknown.

5. Wah and Glen Chang, personal interview, March 26, 1994.
6. Ibid.; "Little Chinese Boy's Etchings exhibited," *San Francisco Call and Post*, date unknown.
7. Wah and Glen Chang, personal interview, March 26, 1994.
8. Ibid.
9. Ibid.
10. Ibid.
11. Barrow and Chang, p. 4.
12. Wah and Glen Chang, personal interview, March 26, 1994.
13. "Chinese Youngster at Age of Eight Puts Name High in Ranks of Child Artists," newspaper unknown, June, 1926.
14. Wah and Glen Chang, personal interview, March 26, 1994.
15. David Barrow, *The Story of Wah Ming Chang*, unpublished.
16. "Kiddies Gang Proves Hit on KFRC," newspaper and date unknown.
17. Wah and Glen Chang, personal interview, March 26, 1994.
18. "Chinese Youngster at Age of Eight Puts Name High in Ranks of Child Artists," newspaper unknown, June, 1926.
19. "Wah Ming Chang Hailed as Genius With Brush; Has Exhibited in Leading United States Cities," newspaper and date unknown.

20. Wah and Glen Chang, personal interview, March 26, 1994.

21. "Fai Sue Chang, Friend of Poor San Francisco Artists, Dead," newspaper and date unknown.

22. David Barrow and Glen Chang, *The Life and Sculpture of Wah Ming Chang* (San Francisco: Sung in Printing, 1989), p. 5.

Chapter 3

1. Wah and Glen Chang, personal interview, March 26, 1994.

2. Ibid.

3. Ibid.

4. David Barrow and Glen Chang, *The Life and Sculpture of Wah Ming Chang* (San Francisco: Sung in Printing, 1989), p. 3.

5. Wah and Glen Chang, personal interview, March 26, 1994.

6. Josephine Whitney Duveneck, *Life on Two Levels* (Los Altos Hills, California: the Trust for Hidden Villa, 1978), pp. 144–145.

7. Barrow and Chang, p. 6.

8. Wah and Glen Chang, personal interview, March 26, 1994.

9. Torben Deirup, telephone interview, July 25, 1994.

10. Ibid.

11. Wah and Glen Chang, personal interview, March, 26, 1994.

12. Torben Deirup, telephone interview, July 25, 1994.

13. Wah and Glen Chang, personal interview, March 26, 1994.

14. Ibid.

15. Torben Deirup, telephone interview, July 25, 1994.

16. Ibid.

Chapter 4.

1. Josephine Whitney Duveneck, *Life on Two Levels* (Los Altos Hills, California: The Trust for Hidden Villa, 1978), p. 149.

2. Ibid.

3. Wah and Glen Chang, personal interview, March 26, 1994.

4. Ibid.

5. "Art of Young Chinese Shows Quaint Humor," *San Francisco Daily News*, date unknown.

6. Wah and Glen Chang, personal interview, March 26, 1994.

7. Ibid.

8. Wah Ming Chang, transcript of audiotaped comments, March 28, 1988.

9. Wah and Glen Chang, personal interview, March 26, 1994.

10. Ibid.; Barrow and Chang, p. 8.

11. Wah and Glen Chang, personal interview, March 26, 1944.

12. Ibid.

13. Wah and Glen Chang, personal interview, March 26, 1994.

14. Ibid.

15. Ibid.

16. Ibid.

Chapter 5

1. Wah and Glen Chang, personal interview, March 26, 1994.

2. Ibid.

3. Ibid.

4. Ibid.

5. Ibid.; Gary Lawrence, telephone interview, July 22, 1994.

6. Wah and Glen Chang, personal interview, March 26, 1994.

7. Glen Chang's response to author's questions of July 31, 1994.

8. Wah and Glen Chang, personal interview, March 26, 1994.

9. Ibid.

10. Ibid.

11. *World Book Encyclopedia* (California: 1983), v. 15, pp. 552-553.

12. Wah and Glen Chang, personal interview, March 26, 1994.

13. Ibid.

14. Ibid.

15. Wah Ming Chang, transcript of audiotaped comments, March 28, 1988.

16. Ibid.

17. Wah and Glen Chang, personal interview, March 26, 1994.
18. Ibid.

Chapter 6

1. Wah Ming Chang, transcript of audiotaped comments, March 28, 1988.
2. Ibid.
3. Glen Chang's response to author questions of July 31, 1994.
4. Ibid.
5. Wah Ming Chang, transcript of audiotaped comments, March 28, 1988.
6. Ibid.
7. "Night and Day," newspaper unknown, December 25, 1940.
8. Wah and Glen Chang, personal interview, March 26, 1994.
9. Glen Chang's response to author questions of July 31, 1994.
10. Wah Chang, taped interview, July 31, 1994.
11. Glen Chang's response to author questions of July 31, 1994.
12. Ibid.
13. Wah and Glen Chang, personal interview, March 26, 1994.
14. Ibid.
15. California Civil code, sections 60 and 69, circa 1942.
16. Texas Penal Code, Article 492, circa 1942.

17. Wah Ming Chang, transcript of audiotaped comments, April 23, 1988.

18. Ibid.

19. Wah and Glen Chang, personal interview, March 26, 1994.

20. Ibid.

21. Hubert Rasbach, telephone interview, July 20, 1994.

22. Wah and Glen Chang, personal interview, March 26, 1994.

Chapter 7

1. J.H. Schoen, "A 16mm. Plea for Peace," *Home Movies* (May, 1947).

2. Ibid.

3. Ibid.

4. Hubert Rasbach, telephone interview, July 20, 1994.

5. Gene Warren, telephone interview, November 29, 1994.

6. Wah Ming Chang, transcript of audiotaped comments, May 6, 1988.

7. Wah and Glen Chang, personal interview, March 26, 1994.

8. Ibid.

9. Wah Ming Chang, transcript of audiotaped comments, May 7, 1988.

Chapter 8

1. David Barrow, written comments, undated.

2. Ibid.

3. David Barrow and Glen Chang, *The Life and Sculpture of Wah Ming Chang* (San Francisco: Sung in Printing, 1989), p. 16.

4. Wah Ming Chang, transcript of audiotaped comments May 7, 1988.

5. *Magill's Survey of Cinema* as quoted in Barrow and Chang, p. 16.

6. Wah and Glen Chang, personal interview, March 26, 1994.

7. Glen Chang, transcript of audiotaped comments, May 8, 1988.

8. Wah and Glen Chang, personal interview, May 26, 1994.

9. Ibid.; Jeffrey Frentzen and David J. Schow, *THE OUTER LIMITS: The Official Companion*, p. 171.

10. James Van Hise, "Wah Chang," *Enterprises Incidents, The Second Star Trek Tribute Book*, (New York: Simon and Schuster, 1988), pp. 59–60.

11. Ibid., p. 172.

12. Ibid., p., 173.

Chapter 9

1. Robert H. Justman, telephone interview, July 25, 1994.

2. Ibid.

3. Ibid.

4. Ibid.

5. Wah and Glen Chang, personal interview, March 26, 1994.

6. Ibid.

7. Ibid.

8. David Barrow and Glen Chang, *The Life and Sculpture of Wah Ming Chang* (San Francisco: Sung in Printing, 1989), p. 19.
9. Ibid.
10. Ibid.
11. Ibid.
12. Wah and Glen Chang, personal interview, March 26, 1994.
13. Ibid.

Chapter 10

1. Wah Ming Chang and Glen Chang, personal interview, March 26, 1994.
2. Ibid.
3. David Barrow and Glen Chang, *The Life and Sculpture of Wah Ming Chang* (San Francisco: Sung in printing, 1989), p. 24.; Wah Chang's response to author questions of July 31, 1994.
4. Ibid.
5. Hank Ketcham, telephone interview, July 22, 1994.
6. Ibid.
7. Ibid.; Wah Ming Chang, transcript of audiotaped comments, May 6, 1988.
8. Hank Ketcham, telephone interview, July 22, 1994.
9. Wah Ming Chang, transcript of audiotaped comments, May 6, 1988.
10. Wah and Glen Chang, personal interview, March 26, 1994.

11. Gary Lawrence, telephone interview, July 22, 1994.
12. Ibid.
13. Ibid.
14. Ibid.
15. Ibid.
16. Ibid.
17. Ibid.
18. "Little Chinese Boy's Etchings Exhibited," Hirsute, newspaper and date unknown.

FURTHER READING

Ames, Lee J. *How to Draw Star Wars Heroes, Creatures, Spaceships, and Other Fantastic Things*. New York: Random House, 1984.

Bandon, Alexandra. *Chinese Americans*. New York: Bradbury, 1994.

Cummings, Pat. *Talking With the Artist*. New York: Bradbury, 1994.

Collodi, C. *The Adventures of Pinocchio*. New York: Macmillan, 1969. (Translated from Italian by Carol Della Chiesa.)

Dillard, J.M. *Star Trek: "Where No One Has Gone Before":™ A History in Pictures*. New York: Simon and Schuster, 1994.

Draw the Marvel Comics Super Heroes. Palo Alto, CA: Klutz, 1995.

Hart, Christopher. *How to Draw Cartoon Animals*. New York: Watson-Guptill, 1995.

Konigsburg, E.L. *From the Mixed-Up Files of Mrs. Basil E. Frankenweiler*. New York: Dell, 1967.

Lightfoot, Marge. *Cartooning for Kids*. New York: Firefly, 1993.

Lord, Bette Bao. *In the Year of the Boar and Jackie Robinson*. New York: HarperCollins, 1984.

Murdoch, David H. *Cowboy: Eyewitness Books*. New York: Knopf, 1993.

Platt, Richard. *Film: Eyewitness Books*. New York: Knopf, 1993.

Raboff, Ernest. *Buonarti Michelangelo*. New York: Doubleday, 1988.

Steele, Philip. *Journey Through China*. New Jersey: Troll, 1991.

Thomas, Bob. *Disney's Art of Animation: From Mickey Mouse to Beauty and the Beast*. New York: Hyperion, 1991.

Viska, Peter. *The Animation Book*. New York: Scholastic, 1993.

White, Tony. *The Animator's Workbook*. New York: Watson-Guptill, 1986.

The World of Theater, New York: Scholastic, 1993. (Expert Reader, U.S. Edition, Dr. Jonathan Kalb.)

INDEX